# CHILD OF THE BLITZ POEMS

By

NORMAN COTTEE

Grosvenor House
Publishing Limited

This book is published by
Grosvenor House Publishing Ltd
Link House
140 The Broadway, Tolworth, Surrey, KT6 7HT.
www.grosvenorhousepublishing.co.uk

A CIP record for this book
is available from the British Library

ISBN 978-1-80381-136-9

Nature abhors a vacuum and I feel that way about blank sheets of paper. I cannot resist idly doodling with a biro and coming up with recognisable drawings of landscapes, aeroplanes, cars, human beings, horses etc. and in a way, metaphorically speaking, this mental urge to create something from nothing allows my muse to touch me on the shoulder from time to time, prompting me to grab my pen if something engages my mind and sets my poetic juices flowing.

This has led over two discreet periods in my life to the composition of fifty three poems reproduced in this volume. They reflect personal and philosophical impressions including places I visited and incidents that have occurred to me from time to time that for some reason have triggered my desire to write once more. It is for others to judge what might have been my precise motivation at the time but I wrote them all simply because I felt the aforementioned urging and hoped that the words I was scribbling on the page would turn out to be pleasing to the ear, stimulating to the mind and warming to the heart.

That said, I have concluded each poem by giving the date when composed and a title giving an indication of the circumstance or impulse that led me to put pen to paper. I wrote my first poems in the nascent years between leaving grammar school in 1959 and becoming a full time, paid up adult in 1961. These eight reflect the pangs of first loves, real and imagined, cold war undercurrents and widening horizons, three of which were included in the magazine published by the St James Church youth club I attended.. They were succeeded in the less frenetic circumstances of retirement by a further 45 poems composed between 2001 to the present day, reflecting a variety of promptings and mortal concerns. At the end of the day, I very much subscribe to the notion that like music, poetry represents the only absolute in a relative world and in this vein, I like to think that my poems in this collection, good or bad, might somehow 'echo round the universe for those who might be listening there'.

# NOTHING TO BE DONE

The tide of time still slinks
Relentlessly from the foreshore
Exposing amid the wastes of sand,
Many coloured pebbles lying
Like basking seals on Arctic reaches:

But here no freshness is,
Only a dowdy dormant haze
Caressing the ripples barely discernible
On the velvet blue of the ocean;
Nothing moves
Nothing goes and nothing comes
As the tenor of life slowly unwinds itself.

To my left the breakwater
Hangs poised as if awaiting
An infinity that it did not care about.
Yet somewhere in this barely breathing vista
Lies the lion that thwarted
Spaniard, French and German in their turn,
That bore our sails to everlasting glory,
That carved this island from Europe's shores
And poured its squealing gallons into the void.
Meanwhile all subsides
The lion sleeps
Mindful of nothing, aware of nothing
...................Till the tide turns.

(Composed and published in 1959 St James Youth Club Christmas
Magazine 'Clubroom' Volume 15 No 4)

# SUBURBIA

These are the streets that know no strife
A handsome life
Love is rife.
From street to street the wiff of hot chestnuts
Binds the municipal.
The cold of the November day
Raises red on cheeks and nose
Activates the brain and numbs the toes.
Now at a given signal
The school doors burst open
Emitting smutty muffled anglo-saxons
Who fling themselves round mothers' thighs
And swot each other with ill-read satchels;
The young order sweep all before,
Mum becomes Mum again
As the first wave establishes itself;
Later, the main body will cross the threshold;
Factory workers, Civil Servants,
Business men, labourers,
Employers and employed,
By bus by train, by tube, by ......
The suburbs loom up
The L T unloads,
The file diverges hurriedly
And all the time the night gets nearer,
Quelle affaire!
But suddenly the world is personal again
And .....
"Hey Mum, it's Dad"

The dog goes mad
"All right!"
"It's time you learned"
"Oh lord that's the second piece I've burned!"
He paces eagerly up the path
And warms himself upon the hearth
A kiss
Then slippered bliss
As the night rumbles up to the French windows.

(Composed in 1959/1960 during my late teens when living at 25 Wolsey Crescent, Morden Park, Surrey in the mock-Tudor semi-detached house my parents named 'Merioneth' in memory of their honeymoon venue)

# AND AFTER THE ATOM

No rest from the ashes
From the torment that is mine,
The barges drift, the engines stand
The cranes lie broken on a hollow land
Pointing to the west
From whence cometh no rest.

All grey day long I drive
The windy vaults of cities piled on cities
And how could I contrive
To change the marble mountains into pity.
You are unaware as I mount the stair
That I am moved -
A pillow and Tchaikovsky's fifth
A burnt cigarette in a dusty room -
A myth,
I am not here at all, nor was meant to be
I shall go down to the river
And drown in the sea.
And welcoming the night
So cool
I wandered through the tombs
And saw
The light of the Eyes
Caught for a moment on a silken screen
Caught between the moment of life
And the moment of death.

Exhausted,
I turned to the City
And the river.
The river is squeezing itself past Tower Bridge
It breathes the frightened air of the Pennines
And it is coming on
Coming on.
Red dust falls by the quay
Red dust by the ditch in which I see
Her footprint still, so small;
A voice behind me dies in flight
And I run in search of the trickling night
By the lonely tree
And the old man's still;
Too true I did not want her then
But now,
Alone in the empty warehouse
I cannot forget.

I have caught the memory of existence
In a jewel
And strapped it on my wrist.
My wrist holds the key to the door
The final despairing twist ......
In the door there is nothing
There is nothing in front of the door
And there is nothing behind the door.
I am alone in a toneless silence
Moving between nowhere and nowhere
In the hour before tomorrow's dawn
Which has never risen
Nor will ever rise.
The river cries softly

And carries my bones to the silver mud
Sifting
Below Gravesend.

The Eyes saw all this,
Digested all this
But I who do not understand,
I have seen the Eyes.
I am not forgotten nor will forget.
I will not forget the Eyes,
I will not forget the City.
Throughout the galaxy only this river still moves.
How can I forget!

(Composed in 1960 during the Cold War for the Trinity edition of
the St James Youth Club magazine 'Clubroom' Volume 16 No2)

# AFTER THE ATOM AFTER-THOUGHT

Down in the tomb where the green grass grows
There lies a lady with marble toes
And on her pregnant belly creep
The insects of the night who reap
The stinking harvest of humanity
So better sleep
Kind mother whom god gave
Unstilted breast yet brain concave
For in your heated bosom lie
Two shining eyes, two shining eyes
Who never wore the wode, yet cry
To break the shell.
Oh hell inside a hell!
Toll the bell, the bloody bell
And if your crumbling fingers
Crumble on the rope
Well who's to blame?
Not fire nor flame, not Jupiter!
Call the first witness
"Name?"
"Er ...Jesus Christ my Lord"
"May I ........"
"Condemned!"
"But why, why .... why?"
Five minutes to go and still I don't know.
You stupid moth!
Can't you see it's all in vain?
Insane!
Do you listen ... insane; ah ha "Sustain"

"Sustain but I'm innocent!"
Chew chew train.
The lights go out
I imagine him dropping
Falling to the floor
For I can see and hear no more
Must I too feed on her belly?
Now my eyes do no more shine?
But I don't see why, unless I ......
"What did he say his name was?"
Unless I ...... (he thinks)
"Pardon?"
"Too late?"
Ah yes, too late (he sighs).


(Composed in 1960 during the Cold War as an addendum to AND
AFTER THE ATOM)

# PEUT  ETRE C'EST FINI

Toujours la même chose
On boit du café
Mont à haut
Voir la cité
Et de loin
La campagne qui rèspire
Et de loin
Le son aigüe
Du train de minuit qui s'envole
Vers le sud.
J'entends partout des cris
Les cris des enfants bleus
À Cassis sur les sables
c'est tout;
Tu était lâ, sous le pont
Jusqu'a la dernière minute.
Je te remercie pour ça
Tu était lâ, c'est tout.

Au clair de la réverbère
Elle regarde ce copain:
Retourne sur ses pas
Sans savoir
Pourquoi je meurs
Parce que ce n'est pas moi
Non plus
C'est la place à Auxerres
Dix-neuf soixante, en hivers.

(Composed in 1960 after summer holiday hitchhiking from Paris
to Cassis near Toulon and into Italy)

# PANTA RE

O bubbly babe how innocence becomes you.
Soon you must appreciate and learn
To wear a bowler hat,
Speak soft phrases, smile and smoke
And be aware of what you are
Or don't you care?

The truth is
I am scared to die
So don't giggle as I squeeze your arm;
The consciousness and experience I now exhume
You must absorb and on it build
Your new creation.

But even you, like me, will never see the light,
It is not for one man to see infinity achieved
For when we reach that state,
By logic or religion,
We become that infinity;
Man ends where the universe begins
And this
The last thing I shall ever know.

(Composed in 1960 and published in the Mothering Sunday
edition of St James' Youth Club Magazine 'Clubroom' Volume
16 No 1)

# THE WASTE SAD TIME

What is this gap
This valley folded,
Where I lie,
Tossing on the sweat of sodden leaves,
Where her smile never smiles
Nor satisfies
But always the phrase recurs
And the sun rises,
I must go down to where
The grass grows thick about my neck
And scratch my legs till the blood
Runs
Freely.
Meanwhile
On this bank I stand
And very cold
Bend to the bitter stream;
The water moves
And she is gone
Into the copse below the hill.
Beautiful the countryside
With the sun through hanging leaves
Bridge moving
Bending its back like strained steel
And a fast tree
Showered
Into atoms on the spiral plain
I can feel the pain of life
Coiled like a spring
Ready to jump
Squeezing a shriek

Here,
Auprès de Lyon,
Where I should have been born
And will die
In a day or two
Under the fringe of a night sky
And my eyes bleed
Till I almost run
To the edge of the morning beating a drum;
An elegant blue
With the unspoken word,
An idea of pink
And motivated genesis?
Slowly the circulation restores
Slimy stone to the fingers' touch;
Between, the pools are clear
And one's thoughts turn to the road
Down which we came.

Touch me
Here now
While I feel my heartbeat
Tearing,
Like a broken prisoner at the gate.
Hold me to the rock.
For we can only be humble
Fishing with the fishermen
Till the day falls
Staring open-eyed
At the sea swell
Talking to the men.

The sun lives here
Moves along

At the back of your neck
Bright burning the Mediterranean houses
White
Into the slow wine hills
Round St Tropez.

And all for me
This little town
Eternal passion
Threaded in the twine of twisting streets
In the shadow shaded by the faded shutter
Where my friends sit
Dark men with brown faces
And barrel eyes
Scarred by salt over ships' bows
And endless summer hours
In the bars along the quay
Consummate sensitivity.
Old women.
Talking of organs and spires,
Desiring only to be left untrammelled,
Undisturbed.

Key turning in the lock
Behind the barred door,
Cold feet on steel sidewalks,
These things I remember more.
Remember me when the shutters close,
Remember me as one of those
Who travelled on the road.

(Composed in June 1961 reflecting overnight ramble in Surrey
Hills and hitchhiking in the South of France)

# RETURN TO ELMER SANDS

I had to go back South,
I felt more
Much more
Than I had before;
South
To Elmer
And the barbeque.
It was dark
Black
And raining.
We kissed,
She moved a breath
Towards me
And in the quiet of the Layne
We touched
Again.

I wish I could feel her like that now
Braced against me
But in the long run
Does it count
That I have loved,
There under the rain,
Does it really matter?
That is what I ask myself.
Can I breathe the sky
Fill the abyss where the thoughts lie?
I would rather build a house
For my kin, than jump off,
Jump in.

And does it matter that I have lived
Here between the light years
Where the fright lies;
Probing restive
Fearing what is and what is not,
Confusion,
Silence,
Of waking to a seamless dawn.

And accepting this or casting it aside
Is the preoccupation of the people,
Who move
Elegantly, always elegantly,
Through the market place,
Down the main street
To the hub,
To Billingsgate in the
Morning minutes.

(Composed in 1961 recalling enchantment when working as a
summer holiday waiter at the Sussex Club, Elmer Sands, Sussex)

# CHINNOR

Cold face,
Starlings in the morning air,
Wheeling, swarming,
Translucent,
Ice stones, meteors;
Unexpected, exposed;
Hit hard, lashing the skin;
Littering the autumn field, sparkling:
Raw red nose and broken plums.

(Composed After Hailstorm at Chinnor Rugby Club in 2001)

# PALEY STREET

Rose-blue, bright sky;
Hint of frost that will come.
Crow dabbling along,
Edging stone grey,
Late spring, warm, woolly
Clouds bear down
On tar macadam not yet melted.
Peat-black, slick crow
Spears the wood where
Bluebell' shimmer sheen
No longer seen.

Heat intensifying,
Plays on the heart and eye;
Mirage in the middle distance,
Mud beyond, horse manure.
Huddled cows in the amber air,
Tail flicking warm flies,
Verdant pastures everywhere.

Detritus dumped disfiguring the landscape
In the gap between low trees and hedge
Lining the verges, marshalling travellers,
Along the road:
Wind brushing the branches
Rushing along
Bending the canopy strongly
On a grey day,
Wet again,
When mortals expect better from their gods.

Already after the rain
Brown stubble ploughed into the dry ground,
Yellowing stalks, broken down, rapeseed rotting.
Horse-high tractors patrolling
The field and lane
Trailing monsters mechanical,
Scattering motorists and seed again.

Solo crow gaining height
Startled feathers jet as night
Flared, fingering the sky in flight
Unaware of risen orb returning
And the field mouse falling
From his hidden house,
Shrill along the sacred way
Scampering, wary, in search of sustenance
While the light holds
And all things ripen into dust.

Grey smudged heron from Babylon
Skims the low flat field
Greets the sun
Seen in winter more,
Now that summer's gone.

(Composed after driving through the Paley Street area in
Berkshire at different times between winter 2006 and late autumn
2007)

# THE VYNE

Four Sea Interludes by Britten,
Peter Grimes, echoing auld measures and modern airs:
Rustic grandeur, shimmering in the late March sunlight.
Wetland and woodland running down to Sherborne St John
Silver birch, lime, acacia and pine
Logs lying; raw carcasses
Piled and strewn haphazardly
Awaiting a better determination;
Felled by wind and man.

In the lake the moorhen and the mouse
Build their nests
Adjoining more familiar brick and stone,
Ruffs from panelled oak look down
Marble busts recognisable and approachable
Pitt the Younger, New Model Protector, Swan of Avon,
In the west wing, three,
Holding quiet sway in people's trust
And my blood moistening;
Regenerating while children play.

(Composed after visit to National Trust Property 'The Vyne' in March 2007)

# AUSCHWITZ-BIRKENAU

I had to come here
In some measure to atone
To this place which has haunted me since I was a boy
And troubles me now I am a man,
A sage of many morning dews.

Shall I send you, grandchild of mine, a postcard?
'Wish you were here' that sort of thing?
Not really; it would not be appropriate,
For the many and the few
Falling into step with desecration,
Passing through.

Strolling through the flat field
Stretching to the near horizon,
Sunlit now, towards the wood,
Empty of numberless, numbered souls
Feather on dry ash falls.

Branded, insured for death on massive scale
Extinguished meticulously, those who fell beyond the pale.
Their suitcases, shoes, spectacles, gold teeth,
Curls of hair, combs, clothes, crutches, brushes, bowls
Consigned to the State,
Not for the vaunted thousand year
But for a bitter moment in recorded time.

Had I been born earlier,
In the land from whence my disposition partly comes,
Tolerating no intolerance, no bigotry, significant or small,
Suffering loss of friends who my name call;

Succumbing, I could have been attendant here before,
Unwitting oppressor in a less transparent time,
Pursuing a flawed dialectic; following a single strand
When there are always many;
Carried round the river bend by currents turned awry,
Too frail to shout to the lone figure
On the far bank standing,
Open mouthed and unable to cry.

'Arbeit Macht Frei' the gate implies:
It's more easy to abhor, more difficult to understand
Where I with the victim and oppressor stand.
Humbling, declining by degree
Degradation, defecation of human flesh
Declining by degree
Beyond all pity be

The guide, who stands by the infamous gate
Has gift of speech and said to us
"I am young. I am alive.
That is all I have. I am happy.
After you leave this place,
Don't think about what you have seen.
Be happy. Life is short; so enjoy it.
Remember only. And goodbye".

I remember.
We are all the few and the many passing through;
Victims and oppressors too.
Chilling it's true. Birds in Birkenau were singing;
And in the adjoining wood, a cuckoo.

(Composed in Krakow, Poland in May 2007)

# UNABLE TO SAVE

In our dreams we exist in a parallel universe,
Without hurt and cost,
Sheltered from the conscious world
Of moments remembered and fleeting time.
Emerging peradventure from the yawning chasm,
The shimmering chimera lost,
We seek succour and recall,
Yet find dismayed,
Naught in cerebral cave awaiting
But message repeated:
File deleted – Unable to Save.

(Composed shortly after waking sometime in 2007 and revised
for photo portfolio in 2015)

# REFLECTIONS FROM A SCENTED ISLE

They say
That when you can see the Isle of Wight
It's going to rain
And when you can't
It's already raining.
By contrast,
In Sicily, when you see the Italian coast
From Taormina,
You know the weather is going to be hot and dry all day
Yet bearable,
But when you cannot see
That rocky toe, thrust like Brutus' dagger
Into the heart of the Mediterranean Sea -
Mare Nostrum or 'Our Sea' as the Romans called it,
Much like we
Call our sea
The English Channel –
When you can't see this southern shore
Shrouded under the Sirocco
Scorching the air, closed in,
The body adapts
By some mysterious mechanism
That harbours hidden capacities
Catering unbidden
With a multitude of unforeseen external changes
To protect the organism;
Mostly unused, not called into play
In this world anyway.

The Greeks say 'Panta Re' – all is change;
And Einstein says all things are relative:
Except perhaps great art and music
As in the last high note that Gladys Knight
Holds in the 'Way We Were'.
Or Mozart played by Alfred Brendel
And the lachrymose of the middle movement of the Concerto for
Clarinet: perhaps that's what music is.
The only absolute in a relative world.
And when we die,
We float away
Into infinity
A fragment of a note
Cast in the teeming air
Souls bare
To echo round the universe
For those who may be listening there.


(Composed during heat wave in Giardini Naxos, Sicily in
June 2007)

# RESCUE ME

What was Lady Penelope's chauffeur's name?
Was it Archibald, Charles or James?
I forget.
Call it advancing senility,
While bustling breezes fly over fruitful Sicily;
And lemons grow.
Ambling through the Corso
In the late afternoon, I remember Virgil and Brains,
Passing caverns of desire
Trading shoes and other riches forged of flame and fire
To which the glitterati aspire.

Shoes - we brought enough
To clad the mighty legions steady tread
And added to our store.
O Virgil, Brains
Come rescue me, before
We pack such chests of treasure
Till they groan
And single-handedly
Extrude
Mount Etna
And the Euro zone.

(Composed in Taormina, Sicily in June 2007)

# A MI PADRE

Sweet fragrance of the light
Green lizard spawning
On basalt stone scorching,
The sirocco
Shrouds the faintly luminescent shore
Where subterranean continents collide
Between Massina and Syracuse,
The ancient city
Where my father lies
In '43, in just such a clime,
Stifled by gun and serge blue,
Where for once, and finally,
The Athenians bought the ruse
No longer fair gifts bearing
To this conjointed state
Or any other within their civilizing gait.

So my father trudged in cause sublime,
A pawn in mighty cause entwined
To join the patchwork teeming soil
To freedom's yolk again, in this fair isle.

How strange that I
Should feel his presence here
And honour him,
When never, he was near.


(Composed in Sicily in June 2007after day trip to Syracuse)

# TO ROSALIND

Rose, hip and jagged thorn, prick the skin,
Cut to the quick, the heart within.
Yet, flared petals, scented sovereign shining,
Justify the mind, replenish the soul,
And make me hope if you be kind,
That you will ever be my Rosalind:
Or if not old and dead, then simply Fred.

(Composed in Celebration of Ros' 65th Birthday at the Waterside Inn in August 2007)

# ODDS FARM

Dressed in blue and grey, pre-school children,
Here for the day.
Polite, engaged, so tiny frames permit,
In jingling line, chattering incessantly,
Jumping, dashing about,
The oddest animals in the farm by far,
Darting this way and that
In some fissiparous pattern,
While the boars, tusks to the fore,
Confront one another and ignore
The facile humans passing.
Yet underneath the facile core,
Values seep in to young minds,
Not created, not imposed
But sending out runners
Seeding themselves,
Randomly
Like wild flowers,
Caught among the briars.

Tolerance, humility,
Eager exploration of new ways,
Fair to fellows:
We choose different words
To cover behaviours
Too diaphanous to photograph or email,
Too ingrained in the land
In which we live and
In the weather.

They colonise minds,
Now and in the future,
The pastures and the cloudy hills,
Towns in the valley
And the cross-roads.

(Composed after visits with Grandchildren to Odd's Farm in Buckinghamshire in Summer 2007)

# THE FLOOD

In the adjacent shire,
Well-meaning, quaint English people demonstrate,
Gathering in the watery lane,
The motley congregation stuttering,
Spluttering and reedy voiced,
Uttering the refrain again and again
'ENOUGH IS ENOUGH'.
Bearing aloft giant letters for the TV crew
'ENOUGH IS ENOUGH' they spell;
Unclear whether to the recent flood referring,
Unwelcome though it is,
Falling within normal parameters
For our latitude and climate,
Or to the warning
Of global warming
Yet to come,
Predicted but not yet proven.

But this is not the death of stoicism.
We are far too polite and reserved for that;
And we love a crisis
That invokes our care
For one another and quiet skills.

And we have a long experience,
Inured in skin and soul, to weather
Surprising us and disappointing,
So that it has become a national passion
To indulge
At the garden fete

The agricultural show and rain sodden barbeque.
But perhaps middle England is right
Standing polite and harmless
Easily ignored, in well used wellies.


(Composed in summer 2007 following heavy rains and flooding in parts of Oxfordshire, Gloucestershire and to a lesser extent in Berkshire)

# OUR LADY OF THE GARGOYLE

Morning dogs at bay
Horses chew the hay
While graffiti artists slink away
In tawdry, teeming old Marseille.
The gargoyle with the bubole guards the harbour
The Vieux Port
Glowering down from lofty perch,
Her wonders to perform
Before the nascent clouds evaporate
And burn away the morn.
The Germans blew up the old quarter
God bless 'em?
And gave the architects, after the war, free rein
To recreate the nouveau quarter
Where tourists wander, bouillabaisse, in concrete blocks
Museums one or two
The old Roman docks remain
Closed on a Lundi.
No rugby neither to watch or play;
We wander aimless
Stunning the local ladies with hirsute tee shirt and shades,
Plastic shoes, buckets and spades
To while away the day.

(Composed in Marseille in September 2007 during the Rugby
World Cup)

# SMALL SIDE

Suffused with bubbling wine
At my niece's birthday celebration,
Drank she still at youthful vigour's overflowing vine
Passing into adult generation.

So it was that long hot summer long ago,
When I was eighteen, I felt aglow;
In my last school year,
No grudging friends' success, nor fear,
No recrimination, nor love ruled out,
No shunning hope in a world of doubt,
But natural, up-swelling, evolutionary joy to be alive,
In dazzling tunes of jazz and jive.

Blazing youth recalling, slipping through the gears,
I haste to meet again the class of '59 and kindred years,
And see, beside the by-pass,
Rock hard for the start of the rugby season,
Now built upon,
The balding patch of grassy pride
We fondly called 'Small Side'
Evoking tousled boys and sterling deeds of yore
Though some be dead or fled to foreign shore.

Remnant in our dotage gathering,
Stumbling, awkward, still hungry for the chase,
We stand in charmless hall and sing,
That peerless old school song and Latin grace.

(Composed in October 2007 following Emily Ware's eighteenth birthday celebration and the 56th Raynes Park Old Boys Society Reunion Dinner)

# CHIMBONDA

Chimbonda, Chimbonda, what a wonderful name;
Not the same when I played the game.
Greavsey, Lofthouse, Mathews, Finney,
Bobby Charlton, Wright Billy;
Hearts of native stock hewn;
Abou Diabey, Kalou now festoon
The soccer scramble in the afternoon.

"What game you watching Lino?" shouts the partisan.
Same as me I would have thought,
As the onion bag twitches in muted retort
And the visiting fans erupt in glee
In the far end pen, sections one through three.
Swelling like a gravity wave, their approbation passes through
The throng around me wearing blue, who blankly stare.
What would they do,
If this were true, plus and minus, transforming of reality,
Not just watching Chelsea versus Villa
In a four all thriller?

(Composed in January 2008 following a Boxing Day visit to
Stamford Bridge to watch Chelsea playing Aston Villa)

# NOUGHTY, NOUGHTY

Nought point nought, nought, three
To nought point nought, nought, six
PSA not Chardonnay.

Railing against the impossible dream,
The clichés tumble out;
I want to shout,
But why the fuss,
When I could get knocked over by a bus.

While I last, I'm going to enjoy these bones
Before my rainbow bubble bursts on ragged stones,
Immersed in the gliding stream, gurgling below laughter,
Rippling and absorbing sodden shoes and socks
Glittering light refracting, weakened at the base of the brook,
Dark newts trail their turgid, narrow tails and ponder other worlds
Not recognised, nor wished for in our blink of time,
By man's invention hewn from the holy sea
Till the last trumpet sounds and casts our alter ego free.

Nothing stays the same except in the memory
Not even in that dusty street in Barcelona
Outside the main station
In the churning heat of an August afternoon
We swoon and wait for the Paris train
Not exactly longing for rain
But dry and listless
On our way home
In former years
To mother's acquiescent tears.

Nothing lasts for ever;
The Sagrada Familia will be finished
But not in my lifetime; not while I'm around.
The paint will faint on the bird's feather
And Gaudi and Miro and Me
Will fire the impossible dream, all three
In the fiery, flaking Spaniards' ground;
For they know all there is to know about death,
When the snorting bull takes its final breath.


(Composed in April 2008 reflecting prostate cancer results, youthful play in the Beverley Brook, Lower Morden, the return journey home from Tarragona in the 1960s and our latest trip to Barcelona)

# PAIN

It's not that I don't care
In the depths of pain
I stand and stare
And cannot drag you out again
From despair into the light.

While you fight to meet
The ground slipping beneath your feet,
Cast adrift in the swirling tide,
You suffer, my bride,
All too soon losing that balance that we know so well,
Descending into living hell.
The well is deep and though we wind and wind,
The heavy bucket weighs and barely rises;
Wrestling and gasping, not out of breath
Lacking understanding, nowhere near death,
When random hours dispose,
Offering scant repose,
The heavy burden of our best endeavours tears apart
The inclination of our heart,
Exhausted, there to find the starless night
Still closed above our head.

As April cedes to May,
Passing by the round-about
Where easing lane slants out,
Bluebells' blush is everywhere;
Profligate, seeding themselves naturally, propagating:
Great survivors of the last Ice Age against all odds.

Oh that we, like them, proliferating,
Might venture forth again in measured song
Toward the new horizon bent
Buoyed by shining throng
And soul inspiring incandescent scent.


(Composed in April-May 2008 during recurrence of anxiety
syndrome suffered by Ros)

# PEACOCK CORNER

Muck and fluckle, buzzing flies
Leaden over blue skies
Down  narrow lane
In deepest Devon, not in Spain
'Our first holiday'
Though we can barely blink,
We will remember it -
Fixed pictures in the memory stick.
Travelling down we slow to a crawl
Passing  Stonehenge, exerting influence still
Traffic piling up along the single road
That sidles past the broad brimmed hill.

I forgot how beautiful it is
This part of the world
Ravishing vistas in every hue
Of green and brown and golden blue
For rain has wrought all summer new
In this secret land
Whose looks can change
In a hair's breadth and whispering sigh
While scuttling cloud and ragged shaft of light
Go scurrying by.

Dimmed, defiant, disappointed, polite
"Say please and thank you children."
Tea in the afternoon
Sipped in delicate china,
Floral pattern preferred to willow;

Devon cream teas
"Yum, yum, scones and jam. Yes please."

"Hello we're from Maidenhead you know
Staying a week."
"We're from Skelmersdale, visiting a cousin
Going home tomorrow."
Much as when Livingstone and Stanley met
In the heart of the Dark Continent
And conquered half the known world,
In stony farmyard, easy familiarity rules;
Animals cluck and adults cackle
Children in verdant valley chuckle.

Delved in high hedgerows
The cockerel crows
Practising his early morning call
And peacock on his self appointed perch, serene
Purveys the scene
And says not much at all.

(Composed in August 2008 during grandchildren's' first holiday
at Knowle Farm near Rattery in Devon)

# RESURRECTION NIGHT

Looking back now, it seems like another world;
Coins in the wheel hubs along the gravel drive;
Our first night together in a double bed;
Dinner at the Frimley Hall;
I can't remember what we ate or drank -
Candlelit over the lake;
Very posh!

Sipping now a biting Sauvignon Blanc,
Succulent, sassy on the tongue,
Fresh from the Isle of the Long White Cloud,
In Cookham, where Sir Stanley Spencer,
Renowned Royal Academician, resigned and reinstated,
Painstakingly resurrection painted,
Plied his idiosyncratic trade,

Soaring above us,
Across the road, from the Bell and Dragon,
Where the wine and Eton Mess is devoured,
The vaulting roof of 'Fernlea',
Blue plaqued semi-detached Edwardian villa
Hard by the river,
Commemorating where Sir Stanley led the middle life,
We wait outside on our betrothing night,
While daughter-in-law picks us up to go back home,
Jane Austen on the telly,
And Mrs Bennett slumbers on the couch:
I said she would!
But what do I know?
We abide and our straggling roots become entangled,

Gnarling year by year,
Comforting and entwining,
In fellowship and amity
And fading threads of familiarity.
Rambling o'er the rug strewn floor,
Knock and bump,
Bibulous in the wee small hours,
We can but slump
And resurrect the morrow,
Open eyed
At that which is to follow.


(Composed  after dining at the Bell and Dragon in Cookham on our 42$^{nd}$ wedding anniversary)

# THE CREDIT CRUNCH

When it finally came, it came, as a shock
As one by one the banks went into hock
To national governments.
And as the patient lay upon the operating table
*"Come back Bretton Woods* if you are able"
Some older heads did cry
The Grande Dame can no more deny
That we are social animals;
Her grocer's bill is paid at last and what is past
Might be retrieved if only we believed
As we did then, in our omnipotence".

Which made me wonder
Where might lie
The eponymous Bretton Woods.
And lo! last night on television,
The answer by and by
Came from Stephen Fry
Whose humble brain the size of Wales
Could raise cathedral questions
And set ablaze
The intellectual aspiration of our age.

In his American tour,
He visits the sepulchral hotel that bears the name,
Sumptuous, vacant, serene,
Of fading fame,
Perched astride the White Mountains,
Broken eons before from Highland chain

Among the dripping heather lain,
Eastward across the Atlantic shore.

And though this edifice was
From a bygone age,
Over elaborate, wildly exuberant, impossibly optimistic,
It served its term:
And we were better for it.
But now the global genie is out of the bottle:
Uncertainty stalks the world
And impending chaos rules.


(Composed in October 2008 at the height of the 'Credit Crunch'
banking crisis signalling the collapse of the post-'Bretton Woods'
era of unbridled capitalism inaugurated by Ronald Reagan and
Margaret Thatcher)

# THE NEW XANADU

Stinking hot in the depths of winter,
I should think not!
Unless you fly to Dubai
Entering a gigantic sand and steel arena,
Thousands of towers soaring heavenwards
Into the blue sky vaulting,
Modern not ancient,
Exuberant, dynamic,
Vast, not beautiful ;
The biggest, tallest building site in the world by far
And more:
Unabashed panache
Striving for the best that cash can buy
So the glitterati and the rich can migrate here,
Yet half of them are fat and ugly
And detritus drifts in the ocean:
Is it a paper cup or can?
Is it a hint that civilisation could be going down the pan?

Dust laden palms blow and cranes rise
To make a Gulf coast spic and span
Sparing no compromise.
For thus has Sheik Maktoum in old Dubai
A stately pleasure dome decreed
Has made the petrol dollars cry
And petrol heads like you and me supply
The warewithal
To forge an Arab kingdom new.
Sustainable?

Who will live and work here?
Will it last the pace of global warming
And man's journey into space?
Waves were gently lapping on this shore
Millions of years before
Cigarettes and tissues lay
Scattered on the sand
By idle human hand displayed.
And though we idly rest and play
In dream hotel and themed designer mall today,
What will become of sifting grains of sand
In the future history of this desiccated land?
The shining steel and glass reflecting boast
May gradually subside to former trading post,
Pearling dhows along the coast.

And when the stars climb into their seat at night,
And the Arabian fox, the wolf and the owl
Hunt once more,
The diminutive mammals, in fright,
In their humble burrows,
Will stifle the twitch and cower
At the sudden omnipotent rush
Of nature's implacable power.

(Composed in November 2008 during a trip to Dubai for the
World Series Rugby Sevens )

# SOMETHING DARWINIAN

I suppose I should write something Darwinian
After all, I'm the only animal among the millions of species
today
Inhabiting this tiny cosmic site
That can write.

Two hundred turns around the sun
Evolving life before and since the great man's life begun,
This archetypal high Victorian English gent
A man of means, by no means indolent,
Assiduous in all he saw and pondered at
Among the jiggelotedy of life and death,
Recognising the random mechanism
By which flora and fauna adapt
Would have readily acknowledged the fact that
At the deepest level, in the quantum mechanical world,
There is no overarching design and
Life follows accident.
]

But our evolved minds think only in terms of reason and of plan
And when we contemplate the heaving strangeness of the
heavens
And the feral forces within them which we cannot see or touch,
We are no wiser than the brittle-backed bugs in bush and rotting
mass,
Unable to grasp the harsh reality of outcomes based on chance
That are neither pre-ordained nor bespoken in advance.

And so I wonder
Whether it is feasible to entertain
The possibility of uncertainty and chance
Operating within a framework
Of orchestrated destiny and dance;
Or, putting it another way,
Is one integral to the other?
A conundrum in a paradox:
An antithesis in an apotheosis.

Bugs will survive us
But does this mean that our mental labours count for nought
When we admire a Shakespeare play
Or, like Darwin,
Uncover new fundamental truths about our world
Revoking sacred doctrines we've been taught?
Religion may have been on the right track once,
But encrusted with titillating thought
And politically fraught,
The idiosyncrasies and illogical leaps of faith
Are too massive, laughable even;
And yet, we stick to them in a passive way,
Vaguely unsure about Charles Darwin
And his panoptic vision,
That leaves us uneasy still,
We who wear the species crown today.

(Composed in February 2009 in celebration of the 250th anniversary of Darwin's birth, after visiting exhibition at Natural History Museum, reading biographies and watching TV programmes)

# TAKING OFF FOR THE LAND OF
# THE FREE (SOUTHERN DIVISION)

Why do I like 'Deliverance' so much?
Because it doesn't pan out in the end;
Something is lost along the way
Never to be recovered.
No happy ending. At best a reappraisal.
Disturbed thoughts remain.

Excited not knowing what to expect
Though Ros and I have been this way before:
Some inconsiderate soul checked in, gone AWOL.
Engines revving, sitting on the tarmac still
While trying to trace the passenger missing
Imaginary or real; terrorist or twit
Perhaps they had a heart attack,
Get those damned bags off quick
Cos I'm getting tense and bored;
I never relax until that mighty thrust
From the Rolls Royce engines forces us
Back into our seats,
Thrusts us forwards, dancing down the blackened line
Flapping upward into the diaphanous air
Banking left, gaining height, soaring rapidly in a large blue sky
Clearing England and Wales in the blink of an eye.

Settle back, relax, enjoy
When the steward comes round
"Cabernet Sauvignon or Bordeaux, Sir?"
Well he doesn't know much about wine,

Which is fine, because I'm up here
And my precious jewels are below;
They will follow me, in time,
Flying the plane or top class passengers at least,
Assuming there is a world to race round then.
But I remain optimistic:
It's in my nature. What else is there?
Always look on the bright side Brian,
Enjoy, enjoy, enjoy.
Shakespeare was more eloquent
But that will do for me,
While waiting for Obama on the White House lawn
Inviting us to tea.


(Composed in May 2009 in Washington DC after flight from London Heathrow)

# FORT SUMTER

Sweltering sun at Sumter
'Fort Sumter'
Mr Rudgeley would intone
In burred brogue that was his alone.
Burly, towering, walrus moustachioed,
Gown flowing
Flown by now,
He made it live for me,
Evoking stories;
His story,
My story of America:
Here he would love to be.

And now our pilgrimage to pay him homage,
Nearly at an end,
We return to Charleston harbour
Round the lazy ocean river bend.

Futile broken walls defended
By the fleeting dream that ended,
Flawed by means unworthy and unfair,
Dignified by valour,
Rebel flag and clamour,
It could not last,
The courteous idyll of an aristocratic caste.

While here and now,
In sleepy southern drawl,
Mighty fine, chill out y'all;
Supine in Savannah, round the pool,
We incline, alpha and omega, shady magnolia,

To England's pretty garden call.
Memorials all, slide into the turbulent past
Into the mouldering dome of memory pall
And gently, while the breeze blown pages fill
With fresh blood spill
In far Iran and home on Henman Hill.


(Composed in June 2009 between Charleston and Savannah, recalling my old history master, Mr Rudgeley)

# THE GOOD SHIP VENUS

Ethereal voices soaring
Into the socket of the masted steeple
Nine hundred years of chastened sound rising;
Bizarrely for a down to earth people.

Minds exulting and the hedonistic heart,
To fly the purity of the thoughts and notes
Into the incandescent air
So that we are carried there,
Locked in a wooded cockpit carved below
In stone-worked starship crewed, for bursting glow
By mortals we attest in time
And launch these hearts in joy sublime,
*'For now we know in part*
*But then shall we know, even as we are known'*;
And the journey starts
That takes us nowhere and everywhere;
Flick the switch, set the sail, timbers caulked in lime,
We rise and sing 'O Come Down Love Divine'.

(Composed in July 2009 on night of Robin and Linda's wedding
service at Chichester Cathedral as they start their voyage together
through married life)

# SUPA SOL

Edeficio Mino, Pooch City.
'Pass me the marmalade'
'Farkinell' - bang, crash,
Blossie through the patio smash.

'Your bathroom stinks.'
Poltergeist, tipped down the sink.
'Flannel sandwich anyone?'
Towel neatly folded on the pillow,
Sunnies inside the cover blind,
Slid inside by tiny fertile mind.

'The ant's not working.' (She's killed it).
'He's resting. Then, when he feels better, he'll go back home.'
'He'll go back to his house in a car?'
'No, ants don't have cars.'
'In a taxi?'
'No, ants don't have taxis.'
'Why?'
'Because they work very hard but they're not as clever as we are
at making things.'
'Why?'

'Hola , Buenos Aires! '
Good time had by all.
Swim, sea, sun, sand, siesta, sangria, sex, – SUPA SOL!

(Composed in September 2009 on return from family holiday in
Guadalmina, Southern Spain.)

# I DON'T KNOW

There is no innate or literal truth in religion,
Including the Christian religion.
But all religions represent,
In one way or another,
The human animal's laudable and poetic attempt
To account for
And come to terms with
The mysterious universe in which we live

Embraced reflectively,
Pursued tolerantly and kindly,
Bewaring the bigot and the Panzer driven zealot,
They are none the worse for that,
Modest and circumspect,
Deserving enlightened support.

But beyond the stained glass fable and the moral call,
I see mainly
Order in disorder,
Disorder in order
Signifying perspectives seemingly more strange and bleak
Than mind's horizon renders weak.

Nor yet have I no deep desire
To divine the divine,
In centripetal black hole
Or anti-matter down the mine.

For me,
It's all right to own,
I don't know.
I feel comfortable with that.
Flesh to cosmic dust that's a fact.
The rest is mystery;
Call it what you will;
Recycled star material.


(Composed in September 2009 after being appointed Sidesman at local church)

# SWEET LASS OF RICHMOND HILL

Bubble-puddled, burnished rubble
Towpath leads beside the sliding river:
Where moorhen bleeps,
Dips beak in meandering deep
And weeps.
But not for me.

Descending whistling whine
Diminuendo of Heathrow plane
As flaps and wheels prepare to come down;
Crossing our way which
Heads for the Star and Garter at the top of the hill,
Centuries old royal residence for wounded men,
Steadfast sentinel commanding
Sullen Thames and sweeping scene.

Tell me Sweet Lass, do you gambol still
Among the speckled daffodil that grow on Richmond Hill?
Bedecked in curlicue,
In arching bonnet, silken ribbon tied,
I glimpse you flitting through the meadow far below
Skipping down the muddy lane, laughing shrill
Frolicking in sandy tree-lined avenue
Beguiling they, like me, who wander will
Round silver-sickled river bend to Kew.

(Composed in March 2011 after visiting Ham House (National
Trust) on the River Thames and completing circular walk along
towpath to, Richmond Hill, returning via King Henry's Mound in
Richmond Park, Petersham Meadow and Ham Polo field)

# CRUISING ON THE NILE

Why are there no ants in Egypt?
Perhaps Rameses thus ordained;
Too dry, too much shifting sand for the little fellows
To build with certainty, their tireless temples and tombs.

Taxi toots, felucca touts dot the Corniche,
Caleche too – Egyptian Ferrari – my name Mohammed, my
horse Susie,
You want to know how much? Five pound for one hour.
Yes, very good price my friend.
Easing barter into banter, promenading at measured pace,
Meandering in the morning hot to the first cataract,
As far as Farouk's Park
The fatty monarch, last of the phoney pharaohs;
And vaunted hotel of 'Death on the Nile' renown
Where Agatha Christie portrayed and stayed;
Simon and Theresa too,
Tea on the terrace,
Don't go to the loo!

The god of fire above, Atum,
Climbs to the height at noon
Glows in the desiccated lapis-lazuli of sky and silver deep of Nile,
Broad reaching artery from which no bile goes
But living water flows.

Finely wrought Nubian silver and semi-precious stones
Clasp slender fingered necks:
Hello, come look in my shop,
Please, come in my shop, look, good price.

The birds have flown at the Aswan Moon;
Duck, 'crammed' pigeon and quail:
We wait, eat, relax  exhume:
Unflustered, while from god of fire below
The ice dust clears
And we fly homeward soon
To muffled cheers,
Friendly remembered waves
And the beat of a clattered drum.


(Composed in April 2010 during a cruise on the Nile between Luxor and Aswan extended due to the eruption of a volcano in Iceland causing cancellation of flights for seven days to and from Britain and much of Europe)

# SOUTH BANK SHOW

At the extreme end
At the end of your tether
Body says lie down
Pride says push on, push on.
Gettysburg and Gabriel's Wharf
Slide beside, the grey and blue-black tide.

What else I see?
Jogger with luminous pants,
Blue lights sprinkled in the tree,
Spindle arches clasping
New Thames Bridge with ease,
Aircraft circling white lights blinking
Gainst the seceding air,
Graffiti cavern, dark and daring
Shading feral kids; no not feral; entertainment free
From grey blocks, reclaiming humour and humanity
Skateboard wizards, flick kick, brave and bare,
It's a cinch, ha ha! go to, go to!
Carried through,
By side door quickly there.

Buzzing crowds pack the unsung Fifties masterpiece,
Twentieth century pieces for us to hear.
Ah Mullova! Viktoria Mullova:
She's the violinist, solo;
She's Czech, she's brilliant.
Not heard of her, no?
Bet you've heard of Victoria Beckham.
She wouldn't know

One end of a violin
From a calf skin handbag; bless her
Little cotton socks. Won't knock;
But how I long for Viktoria, my Viktoria
And a sip of high blown unabashed, high brow,
Heart and mind inspiring cultural tea.
And it's being recorded on the BBC!

Music moves me most,
Although the British Museum today came close
A real eye opener.
High minded culture isn't dead you know,
Despite the demise of the TV South Bank Show.
No sah! No, no, no.
It's just the proles have taken hold of
The megaphone right now.
Push on, push on!

(Composed in February 2010 after British Museum & Royal
Academy Van Gogh Exhibitions, Enjoying a meal at the Italian
Restaurant at Gabriel's Wharf on the South Bank, reflecting on
the passing river and the Battle of Gettysburg in the American
Civil War, before attending a Concert at the Royal Festival Hall
on the South Bank)

# LAST TRAIN TO SAN FRANCISCO

All aboard; reserved
From the top deck viewing, only
One step up from shacksville - trailertown;
Even the better homes are packed together,
Small back yards
Where little scrubby grass grows,
Dereliction: overhead wires
Supported on poles tall as California palms
Lacing straight wide streets
In which the shiny automobile
And pick-up truck is definitely king;
Tasteless cheese and horseradish sauce smother everything
Gouging gently garnered crab round Frisco Bay:
Discarded cars and industrial plant betray
Huge means and vast capacity
Made manifest around LA.

At the farthest bend of the longest day
In Yosemite, in matchless beauty, the black bears play.
Fresh morning, hot and blue,
The Amtrak whistle blows,
Fast train for Bakersfield on Track Two.
Hurry folks!
In the arid, irrigated, sun drenched plain,
Fruit, nuts and vines not yet in harvest trim
Stretch for miles and miles and miles
To the Sierra rim.
Dead machines in the Mojave abandoned stand
Bonnets and boots gawping toothless

Like Ozymandias in the sand
Awaiting the new creation
And the destruction of all land.
Meanwhile arise!
The new Jerusalem, the fantasy and flash
Where humans throw away each day, millions of paper cups and
trash;
Each day the mindless drain of dice unheeded thrown,
Of the chance to win
And make it back another day
To lose and cling
To the American dream
Of being nice and owning everything
So long as it's bigger, wider, taller bling
Not factoring,
The quality of a Monet, Hockney and Sisley too
Or the perfection of a vase by Ming
Unless that is you're bold enough
To brave the clinking miasma of the casino cave
To seek and find the cultural stuff.

What's happening?
This place is beginning to grow on me;
A few more outdoor restaurants, gardens and park benches
And I could stay longer
Here in the desert spring
But the whistle blows for Hoover Dam and Arizona,
Red Indians and Cowboys tall
To the Grandest Canyon of them all;
Till it's time to board the midnight train
To El Pueblo de Nuestra Senora de Los Angeles
A merry night of stress and strain,
Cooped up, confined, like Boris Becker with his dusty maid,

Without the thrill of coitus made.
But we pull through;
We're British don't you know!
Put it down to expear...iance
So have a chuckle
And in the panelled ballroom of the Longbeach 'Queen'
Let's dance.
In graceful retirement, we salute you, Mary,
Recalling past imperial glory,

Then back we go along the coast,
To embrace the wisdom of the mighty redwood tree,
To sidle through Carmel and El Grande Sur;
Dolphins glide, nonchalant and free
O'er wave and spray,
To calm our skins and pass the hours in sparkling Monterey;
For we're going back to San Francisco,
In another place and another time,
To meet our people there:
For our end to our Great Rail Journey
And to the end of my rhyme.

(Composed in June 2011 during Great Rail Journey through
California, Nevada and Arizona on the West Coast of the United
States of America travelling from San Francisco via Merced in
the central valley, Yosemite National Park, Bakersfield, the
Mojave Desert, Las Vegas, Hoover Dam, Williams, Grand
Canyon, Los Angeles, Hollywood, Beverley Hills, RMS Queen
Mary at Longbeach, returning to San Francisco via Pebble Beach,
the Big Sur and Monterey)

# FALLING DOWN

John, John, what hast thou done?
Douglas lies abed,
Crown of thorns, slipped aslant,
Pearl pricked on his head.
I bring the magician's broken wand
But have no faith in voodoo patterned wood.
My friend, you're looking good,
Your glad eye glazed, searching somewhere distant,
Recollecting perhaps, the ground lost amidst the smoke and
thunder of the storm;
Buckling body falling down
Under the sullen silence of the grey flecked, vaulting sky
Flowing above and beneath us,
Purging epiphany in the dissolving rain
Your very own 9/11.
Random number in a random world
Where suffering and ineffable beauty co-exist,
Where even the terrible destruction of the tall towers crumbling
Has a dreadful beguiling motion,
Against the serene blue of a Manhatten morn.

And here am I,
Knowing not what to say or what to pray for, how to be.
It's a bugger.
Friend, friend – te amor:
Rise up and follow me.

(Composed in September 2011 around the time of the
10th anniversary of the 9/11 terrorist attack on the USA, following
the collapse and hospitalisation of my friend John Rees - official
first name Douglas - due to bleeding in the brain,)

# OVER AND OUT

We all die unperfected;
Lives unperfected
Careers unperfected
Relationships unperfected;
Imperfect seeing eyes,
Imperfect cavernous ears
Declining the sweetly knelling bell of boundless youth
Undimmed by disappointment, envy, shame:
Paying the price that partial wisdom partly pays
For gnarled experience, creaking limbs and memory's faze.

On we go, unperturbed;
On towards the green and chalk white ridge,
Steeped in purple autumn mist, we go
Casting dust and stuff behind the funeral cars,
Lie we low,
Enclosed in loam,
Touched from head to toe by nightly mole.
And up above,
The modest cowslip turns its pretty petalled head
To communicate with stars
The sad news;
Uninspiring, unsurprising, no less significant,
No more devout
Than the press of rustling zephyr on lacy wing,
Reverberating from flint stone chapel
Where the choir and congregation sing -
"Earth to earth, dust to dust, ashes to ashes"
"Over and Out".

(Composed in September 2012 inspired by Stubbings Church and
churchyard)

# SCUTARI

Here am I, in Ward 4 waiting,
Waiting, waiting,
At the military hospital at Ascot,
Built by the British for the plucky British Tommy and their
officers,
In time of war;
Waiting for my body to be stretchered forward
To the operating theatre,
Missing the consolation of 'going over the top',
Low-rise, ramshackle conglomeration of huts and buildings;
The better to be close to the receiving earth;

The wind howls outside,
History of the Crimean War by my side.
But for the intervening years
I would have lain among the wounded,
Waiting, waiting;
Injured mortally perhaps, waiting for Godot;
Passing concluding moments with a gentle sigh,
Ignorant of the miracle of modern medicinal science:
Scutari in the present tense:
Sweet lullaby.

(Composed in February 2014 in Ward 4, Heatherwood Hospital,
Ascot, while undergoing hip replacement surgery-Dedicated to
Oliver & N'eve who talked to me about hospitals and Scutari in
the Crimean War).

# THE WHITE FEATHER

I don't really believe in supernatural stuff:
But it was odd.
A white feather descended into the sunken patio
And lay there; offering a kindly message from Charlie that he
had just left this life
And was happy.
A few moments later, when we looked again, the downy
messenger had departed
Leaving the patio silent and empty as before.

As Austin said, the next day;
'Charlie was in cat heaven with his cat friends and had Wins.'
"Wins?"
Shouting loudly into my ear – "Wins....Granddad ....Wings"
"Oh Wings!"
"You mean like angels;
"So he can fly where he wants among the stars and planets in the
universe."
"Yes that's right."

Though forged in ash anew,
No longer in my sight,
I like to think that's how it is,
Because I miss him still,
Both day and night.

(Composed in March 2014 following the death of Charlie, our
family cat for nineteen and a half years)

# DEMON BARBERS I HAVE KNOWN

I've known some demon barbers in my time;
Chris Barber, the jazz band leader of 50s fame,
Samuel Barber, the composer,
The singing Barber of Seville, no less
And Sweeney Todd, of course,
The most demonic of them all
To name but a few
And not to mention Medusa, in Ancient Greece
Who had a bad hair day
That lasted centuries, nay millennia;
Writhing, hissing serpents sprouting from her crown;
And instead of cutting off her slithey mop
Young Perseus saved the earth by chopping off her top.
Nor wiley-smiley Delilah
Who sapped young Samson's strength
For a paltry golden crock
By snipping from his top
His seven stranded lock.

But I swear....
None will compare
With the fair maid of Maidenhead.
She clips them here, she snips them there,
She sculps the bonce a treat
For in the scissor swizzling trade, there's none so reet,
As can surpass all rivals near and far,
Tis but the queen of curls -
The Brill Close Nicola!

(Composed in December 2014 in recognition of my hairdresser
par excellence Nicola Cottee)

69

# THE LEATHERN PASS

I know it's daft
And I know that you have moved and lived
Away from here before now; far and wide,
But I can't help feeling
That this time
A cord has been snapped, though others hold
And a rite of passage transcended.

Don't laugh.
Or laugh a little or a lot.
It matters not
A silent suppressed smile
Softly surfaces from somewhere inside of me:
Consoled I be.
You and your family
Are alive and have achievements lying before
While time passes gently behind me now,
Beat by beat;
And it really doesn't matter.
That when I make my final play,
Contented I shall lay
In the receiving earth from whence I came.

My grandsons ask me
Whether I am proud of you.
What do you think?
With all you have achieved
And will achieve withal,
I rest easy, pray for you.

But don't pray for me to any murdering god.
Just garner our memory
And care for our remembrance
Mumsy and me.
For I have given you the leathern pass
In space and time
And know that you will run it home
Triumphantly.

Meanwhile, I'm writing this in the small hours
For my sins,
After first viewing Shelburne House:
C'mon You Quins!

*(Composed in March 2017 after having viewed Phil and Nicola's
new house in High Wycombe in the hours when the clocks went
forward)*

# THE CIRCLING SEA

Is it the weather that binds us together,
Or is it the circling sea?
Following the vote,
You know what;
I don't much care;
And rather despair.
For where are the Spinozas of yesteryear
Who see beyond the self absorbing prejudice
Of fish and chips and petty fear?
Who will the standard bearer be
For decency, for humanity,
For the planet as a whole,
For the butterfly on translucent wing
That speciates, yet flowers all?

Cromwell, Churchill, Alfred, Lincoln tall
Why answer ye not my call?"
For no village Hamden ere the close of day
Strides past me on my winding way
Along the pure and simple path
To home and warming hearth!

(Composed in July 2017 as the misbegotten Brexit negotiations
begin)

# THE LAST OF THE ARBERS

O fair of face
At rest beneath thy 'Loveliest Tree'
Grant us thy grace
In every breath
To praise and honour thee.
Could we but resurrect
Those favoured times
In 'Heimat' now,
Thy tender mien and dulcet tone;
The vanished world we deemed our own;
We would cherish and remember
And tell such tales
That would make us laugh and cry.
For we are fragile beings
Yearning to be characterful and true,
Aspiring to be granite rocks like you

(Composed in August 2018 on learning of the death at the age of
98 of my Aunt Dorothy, the last of my mother's Arber generation)

# GUERNICA

In the Botanical Garden,
Lime green parrots saw
Between the trees and caw,
Jostling presiding maestro magpies
On the fountain bowl.
A sudden shower unexpected
Drenches and dries the pathways and plants
While undisturbed, the traffic hums;
Stone statues of city worthies silent remain:
A poet maybe, seed monger, contented gardener,
Disregarded, well reported in their day.

Along the gravel path
Mushrooms sprout like tea trays
From the elegant trunk
Of a majestic Elm tree hulk;
Victim of beetle born disease
Remarkably, though long dead,
Sustaining life still,
Showing how resilient nature is.

In the hotel rooftop restaurant
Dinner reservation annulled
Because of the sudden storm.
*"I'm sorry to disappoint you...bla.... bla...."*
Well intentioned, kind
*"Not your fault"* I say
*"We're English; we crave disappointment".*

Down to the usual venue on the corner
Of the pretty square
Next to the hotel entrance.
A lovely appley rueda verdejo
And Premier Cruzcampo.
Better meal, better atmosphere,
More Euros to jangle in mein poche:
Old Joes better by far than rooftop bar.
We talk to a Swedish Londoner
His English is impeccable
And guard his Iranian girlfriend's handbag
For a while:
They live together in London
And love Madrid.
Young love? I hope so.
And successful, I hope so.
"Goodnight; have a good night"
"See you in London sometime"

The wind gets up,
The candles shudder.
Reminds me of home
"Turned a bit chilly"
Back to the hotel
Only a night beat stride away
At the end our Guernica gallery day.

(Composed in September 2018 after visiting the Reina Sophia
Art Gallery in Madrid to see Picasso's famous 'Guernica'
painting)

# LANTIVET

For The past few days
For reasons I shall return to later
I have felt a subconscious urge to write another poem;
Only a slight but persistent urge mind you
Of the lurking kind that won't go away:
I don't honestly have the time at the moment
But will come back to it.

Today I learned something new
During the course of our brain tumbling walk
Across the unkempt field
Trespassing, strictly speaking, on Great Western property,
Towards the footbridge carrying Breadcroft Lane
Across the railway line connecting London City
With the far reaches of Cymru and the ragged tip of Cornwall
Land's End folks, end of the line,
And nought thereabouts but passage for the Americas sign.

Anyway, finding it too much for limbs arcane
To vault or somehow climb the fence
Into the aforesaid Breadcroft Lane,
We returned the way we came,
Passing a silent stranger, harbouring an unknown quest,
Benign or malevolent it was impossible to guess;
But rather than returning homeward bent our way
Towards Woodlands Park
Along the linking road
Flanked by modest bungalows
Bordering the grassy airfield;
Completely transmogrified over the years

Since their nativity during the war.
Yet one had remained unchanged, forlorn, forgotten
In contrast to the prevailing embellishments and extensions,
Half-hidden, a stone's throw from the most transformed of all;
A Neo-Georgian mansion bounteously bordered;
Sporting obligatory classical statue
Ostentatiously mounted on meticulously, manicured lawn.
And the name of this imposing, incongruous residence,
Was 'Lantivet'.

Today I learned something new
Although I had always known it:
That Lantivet is Cornish not Welsh as I thought;
Albeit the two languages have a common root;
And means 'cultivated valley'.
Now Woodlands Park can only loosely be termed a 'cultivated valley'
The predominant feature of the landscape being flat
So I surmise that
The owner of this imposing pile
Was not raised in this locality
But in Celtic Cornish extremity
Linked by human footfall o'er ten thousand years
And by railway now,
Where we stumble quite by chance
Embedded in this modest corner
Preserved, alive and clarion caller,
A living vestige of our pagan past.

(Composed in October 2018 after a therapeutic walk with my wife in the local area)

# LAKE LUGANO

No I don't want to write a poem now
Although the leaves fall
And it's not autumn at all:
Casting three coins in the waters
For my classmates Tim, Peter and Derek
No longer with me:
Biddiscombe, Williams and Furminger.
With me in the age of innocence;
Here with me in 59
By the banks of the lake,
And the town much changed
Over the passage of time

I hear the coins plop
Rattle of machine gun fire in the pond,
Recalling what was before
And what is now

Another leaf is about to fall,
Not with me in the Swiss Lakes then
But long lasting school friend all the same;
Not in my year but in the same House
Who may not see another spring:
Stevenson - Robbie
And I alone shall stand,
Apart from French - Terence that is,
The last trumpet in the Raynes Park band.

In the twinkling of an eye we live and die,
Precious flesh, sentient and endearing,
We strive to understand; some good try;
Flare briefly in the enveloping darkness.

But hey Jeromino!
It was fun though;
While it lasted.
We felt, we imbibed, we loved,
We sought, we observed, we found:
And now we lie well tempered in the ground.


(Composed in April 2019 after returning from a holiday in Lake Como, including a nostalgic day trip to Lake Lugano, the location of a memorable Raynes Park Grammar end of term school holiday in 1959)

# CELLULITIS

On our last night in the villa
An insect, or something similar,
A vampire perhaps; I don't know.
Punctured my leg from knee to toe,
Allowing dangerous microbes in,
Suppurating flesh and skin,
Home from France,
Threatening life perchance;
Cellulitis the medical name;
To Wexham Hospital I came.

Hazily in Ward Six curtained, corner bed
Through portals high above my head
At summer's burning sun I gazed,
Might this be where I end my days?

Insidious dreams portending last rites,
Disperse reassuringly in ensuing nights,
Allowing progressive recuperation,
Surprise and welcome visitation
From daughter-in-law and mother.

We hold venerable hands
Her mother and I
She in her wheelchair beside my bed,
Comforting one another,
Joshing and reminiscing,
Acknowledging without words
As old people do,
A shared mortality.

And I thought how fit and alive
She looked and sounded;
Drole, vivacious, a sparkle in her eyes,
We laughed and determined.
Said our goodbyes,
Wished each other well.
And two days later,
From the hospital I walked free
But not she.

Travelling home following her visit
Suffering a sudden relapse
From a previously diagnosed heart condition,
She returned to the hospital
And died not yards from me
In Acute Ward Three,
Cold to the touch,
Of those who loved her so much.

Freed at the last from daily toil,
Embalmed in Berkshire soil,
A bard from native Emerald Isle,
Prompted these words of prayer:
That under spreading green oak tree
In tranquil Braywick cemetery,
She rest contented ever there
In treasured memory.

(Composed in October 2019 after recuperating in Wexham Park
Hospital from a potentially lethal bacterial infection, while
coincidentally witnessing the demise of my daughter in law's
mother there)

## *BE GONE DULL BOY*

And so it is and so it's been
Four score years and loss of friends have seen.
Marking out the pegs
Straining on old legs,
Slippering me softly to the fulcrum hour,
Where silver bearded  sickled power
Parading on the last horizon stands,
Beckoning me, calling me,
Begone dull boy
And set me free.

(Composed in April 2021 approaching my 80th birthday)